HOW TO STRENGTHEN YOUR FAITH 2.0

"Stand firm in the faith."
—1 CORINTHIANS 16:13

STAN TOLER

dustjacket

Dust Jacket Media Group
PO Box 721243
Oklahoma City, OK 73172
Info@DustJacket.com
Printed in the United States of America
ISBN: 978-1-947671-33-1

Writer: Stan Toler with Kevin Riggs

This Bible study is a companion book to Stan Toler's *Total Quality Life: Strategies for Purposeful Living*, expanded ed. (Indianapolis, Ind.: Wesleyan Publishing House, 2009).

CONTENTS

WEEK 1
PRAISE

RECOMMENDED READING

Total Quality Life, chapter 2, pages 19–26; chapter 6, pages 83–85

Christian thinkers from Augustine to Pascal have described an emptiness that is found in every human being which can only be fulfilled in relationship to our Creator. You can guard your thought life, improve your health, and watch over your finances, but if you don't place your faith in God and grow in your faith, then all the rest will matter little. Jesus said, "What good is it for a man to gain the whole world, yet forfeit his soul? Or what can a man give in exchange for his soul?" (Mark 8:36–37). The apostle Paul put it this way, "For physical training is of some value, but godliness has value for all things, holding promise for both the present life and the life to come" (1 Tim. 4:8). While every aspect of total quality life—thoughts, health, finances, faith—is important, none is more important than faith.

The apostle Peter wrote, "But grow in the grace and knowledge or our Lord and Savior Jesus Christ" (2 Pet. 3:18). What are some things you can do to grow in your faith? Over the next few weeks, you will learn six ways to increase your faith by focusing on praise, prayer, thanksgiving, meditation, fellowship, and ministry.

Let's get started with growing in your faith by cultivating a life of praise.

DAY 1

Psalm 150:1–6

If someone asks you to look for something blue, what happens? The color blue suddenly seems to pop out everywhere. Then, if the person asks you to look for things that are red, the blue gets lost and the red starts to jump out. Is this a trick to make you see things that are not there? Not at all. The colors are always there, even if you don't notice them.

Likewise, God is all around you. He can be seen in the everyday activities and interactions of an otherwise mundane routine. The question is not whether God is there; it's whether you're going to take time to focus on him.

Praise is the theme of Psalm 150. Thirteen times the writer tells us to praise God. The Hebrew word translated *praise* is *halal*, from where we get our English word *hallelujah*. The word *halal* means to make clear, to make a show, to boast, to rave, to celebrate. You and I are to make a really big deal about God! Not only are we to praise God at church ("in his sanctuary," v. 1), but we are also to praise him in creation and because of his power and greatness (vv. 1–2). We are to praise him with instruments, dancing, and resounding cymbals (vv. 3–5). Our songs of praise should be exciting and moving, not dead and somber. Through our praise, we proclaim who God is and what he has done. Our praise involves every aspect of our lives. "Let everything that has breath praise the Lord" (v. 6).

Begin focusing on God and praising him and you will see him everywhere and at work in everything, which will make you praise him even more. Are you living a life of praise?

QUESTIONS FOR REFLECTION

1. How would you define praise?

2. What do you think is the difference between praise and thanksgiving? Is there a difference?

3. Can you make a list of ten things for which God is to be praised? (Hint: The ten things should be all about God, not about what God has done for you.)

PRAYER FOR TODAY

Praise the Lord! O great God of heaven and earth, I give you praise. You are worthy of all my praise. My prayer today is that my life would be a praise offering to you. May all that I do and all that I am bring you honor, glory, and praise. In Jesus' name I praise. Amen.

DAY 2

ISAIAH 6:1–13

A great way to praise God and grow your faith is to think about his many characteristics. Over the next four days, we are going to look at four key characteristics of God. The first characteristic, and the most foundational, is his holiness. Before God is anything else, he is a holy God. Isaiah gives us a remarkable picture of God's holiness.

After a reign spanning fifty-two years, King Uzziah died from leprosy in 739 B.C. During that year, Isaiah had a vision in which he was ushered into the heavenly throne room of God. What most overwhelmed Isaiah was God's holiness.

"Seraphs" (v. 2) are a type of angelic creature who worship and serve God. The seraphs Isaiah saw had six wings. Two of the wings were used for flying. The other four wings illustrate the holiness of God. Two wings covered their feet because the throne room was holy ground (see Ex. 3:5). Two wings covered their faces to prevent them from gazing directly into the face of God's glory (see Ex. 33:18–20).

The seraphs were calling out to one another, "Holy, holy, holy is the LORD Almighty; the whole earth is full of his glory" (v. 3). As the angels sang their song, everything "shook and the temple was filled with smoke" (v. 4). God's holiness is majestic, glorious, awe-inspiring, and frightful. He is to be feared, praised, and worshiped.

The moment Isaiah came face-to-face with God's holiness, he immediately saw his own sinfulness (v. 5). But one of the seraphs took a live coal, similar to what a priest would do on the Day of Atonement (see Lev. 16:12), and cleansed Isaiah, taking away the guilt of his sin

(vv. 6–7). When people have real encounters with God's holiness, they are moved to truly repent, and God is moved to completely forgive their sins.

Having truly repented of his sins and received forgiveness, Isaiah was motivated to serve God, regardless of what was asked of him. Likewise, God has something for you to do. God has placed a calling on your life, and only you can do what he has called you to do. Are you willing to do it? Are you willing, like Isaiah, to say to God, "Here am I. Send me!" (v. 8). If you have truly encountered God's holiness, repented of your sins, and received forgiveness, what else can you say?

QUESTIONS FOR REFLECTION

1. What do you think it means to say that, before God is anything else, he is holy? How would you describe God's holiness to someone else?

2. Has there ever been a time when you experienced God's holiness? Has God ever revealed himself to you? What happened? Did you repent?

3. What do you believe God has called you to do? Are you willing to do it?

PRAYER FOR TODAY

Dear God, words cannot adequately express your holiness. You are a holy God, and that alone means you are worthy of my praise. In light of your holiness, I recognize my own sinfulness. Forgive me. Take away my guilt. Almighty God, in response to your forgiveness, I commit my life to you and will do whatever you ask me to do. In Jesus' name I pray. Amen.

DAY 3

1 JOHN 4:7–12

People often describe God with the saying, "God is love." You could easily get the feeling that God is the grandparent in the sky: God loves you so much that he would never tell you no; he will always give you candy; and he is a whole lot nicer than your parents. It is precisely because of this misconception about the love of God that you have to start with God's holiness. God is love, but he is holy love.

John told us that we are to love one another, and he suggested that apart from God, a person cannot really love others. John's logic was simple: (1) since God is love, love comes from God; (2) if you have a relationship with God, you will love other people; and (3) if you do not love other people, you do not know God (vv. 7–8).

What does it mean to say God is love? Far from being a grandparent who chooses to look the other way when grandchildren do wrong, God's love motivated him to send Jesus into the world to die so we could be forgiven of our sins and brought back into a right relationship with God. For John, the remarkable thing was not that we love God; rather, it was that God loved us (v. 10).

Because God is a holy God, he cannot coexist with sin. God's holiness requires sin to be punished. Since God is an eternal being, the holy and just punishment for sin is eternal death—eternal separation from God.

But since he is also love, God, an eternal Being, became a man, a mortal being. Jesus, God in the flesh, was able to pay the eternal punishment in a moment of time by dying on the cross, paying our penalty for sin. Thus, in and through Jesus Christ, the holiness of God was satisfied, the love of God was demonstrated, and through faith in him, you and I are justified.

Yes, God is a God of love, but the crucifixion of his Son shows us that his love is a holy love, and his love is utterly amazing. Therefore John concluded, "Since God so loved us, we also ought to love one another. No one has ever seen God; but if we love one another, God lives in us and his love is made complete in us" (vv. 11–12).

QUESTIONS FOR REFLECTION

1. What do you think it means to say God is love? How would you describe the love of God to others?

2. How did the death of Jesus on a cross satisfy God's holiness and demonstrate God's love?

3. In what ways should God's love for us motivate us to love one another?

PRAYER FOR TODAY

Dear God, I am humbled by the fact that you love me. Before I was even capable of loving you, you loved me. I praise you for your love. I praise you for your mercy and compassion. I praise you for Jesus Christ, and it is in his name I pray. Amen.

DAY 4

HEBREWS 4:13–16

The writer of Hebrews had some difficult things to say, including warning his audience against disobedience. One day we will stand before Almighty God to give an account of our lives (v. 13). On that day, there will be nothing to fear if we have placed our faith in Jesus Christ, because he is our "great high priest" (v. 14). Jesus entered the very presence of God ("gone through the heavens," v. 14), who accepted his sacrificial death on the cross. Jesus' work had been completed. Nothing more needs to be done for our salvation. All we have to do is accept the finished work of Christ by faith.

Jesus is our great high priest because he knows what we are going through. He knows our weaknesses and has been tempted in every possible way, but he never gave in to these temptations. He never sinned (v. 15). Jesus had to be God in order to have the power to die for our sins, but he had to be man in order to have the right to die for our sins. Because of the life, death, and resurrection of Jesus, we can "approach the throne of grace with confidence, so that we may receive mercy and find grace to help us in our time of need" (v. 16).

Twice in verse 16, the word *grace* is used. The Greek word translated *grace* is *charis*, meaning a kindness, or favor, given to someone who does not deserve it. The first time *grace* is used in verse 16, it is described as a characteristic of God. He is the source of this undeserved kindness. For the believer, God's throne of judgment becomes a throne of grace. The second time *grace* is used in this verse, it is described as a gift God gives believers to empower them to live every day. The second usage is partnered with the word *mercy*. If grace is getting something you do not deserve, mercy is not getting what you do deserve. The first type of grace is saving grace; the second type is sustaining grace. And we need both even though we deserve neither. God is gracious, and in the same way we receive eternal life by his grace, it is also through his grace that we receive strength to live in this present life.

QUESTIONS FOR REFLECTION

1. How do you think you will feel when you stand before God to give an account of your life?

2. What do you think it means to say Jesus is your great high priest? How would you explain what that means to others?

3. How would you describe the difference between saving grace and sustaining grace? Why do you think both are needed?

PRAYER FOR TODAY

Dear God, I praise you for your grace. Without it, I would be lost in my sins. Without your grace, I would have no hope in this present life. Your grace is amazing. Your grace is beyond my comprehension, but I place my faith and trust in your grace, through faith in Jesus Christ. I pray all these things in Jesus' name. Amen.

DAY 5

Psalm 115:1–18

The emphasis this week has been on growing your faith by living a lifestyle of praise. We offer God thanks because of what he has done. But we praise him because of who he is. He is Almighty God. He is holy, and he is full of holy love and holy grace. God is also to be praised because he rules over all creation. He created all, knows all, and sustains all. It is because of his authority over all things that he can be trusted in all things.

Psalm 115 is in the middle of a six-part series of praise psalms. These praise psalms were used in many of the Israelites' festivals and holy days, but were primarily used during Passover. Psalms 113–114 were usually sung before the Passover meal; Psalms 115–118 were usually sung after the Passover meal.

We live in a day when fame and fortune are celebrated, but God alone is worthy of our praise and worship. To those who choose not to believe, God seems absent. But for those who believe, God is everything. "Our God is in heaven; he does whatever pleases him" (v. 3). This would be a scary thought if not for the fact that God is loving and faithful (v. 1). Whatever God chooses to do is right, just, and holy. God is the one and only God. All other supposed gods are nothing more than objects made by man that can neither speak, see, hear, smell, feel, nor walk (vv. 4–7).

Almighty God is a personal God who does speak, see, hear, smell, feel, and walk. He is in control; he can be trusted. He is our "help and shield" (vv. 9–11). Both terms, *help* and *shield*, are military terms.

Someone who helps is an ally, and a shield is used for protection. When you and I place our trust in God's power and authority, we have nothing to fear, because God is our ally—he will stand with us against our enemies—and he is our protection. We can trust in God because he has promised to bless all who believe in him (vv. 12–13). Everything belongs to God, and he deserves our praise. It is only wise to trust in him.

Do you want your faith to grow? Then give God praise in all things and trust in his loving, faithful reign over all of life. He knows the future, as well as the present and the past. Nothing has ever caught him off guard. Things may seem chaotic, but God is still in control. In an ever changing world, he is the only thing that doesn't change. He is powerful; he is holy; he is love; he is grace. Praise his name! Focus on him and you will see him in all things.

QUESTIONS FOR REFLECTION

1. How do you think living a life of praise will increase your faith? Are you living a life of praise?

2. In what ways would trusting in God's sovereignty increase your total quality life? What do you think it means to trust God's sovereignty?

PRAYER FOR TODAY

Dear God, I praise your holy name. You are a God full of love and grace. You have all authority. You alone deserve all glory. Praise your name. I pray that I will live a life of praise. Thank you for loving me and for reminding me this week of who you are. I love you. In Jesus' name I pray. Amen.

WEEK 2

PRAYER

RECOMMENDED READING

Total Quality Life, chapter 6, pages 86–88; chapter 8, pages 132–136

God is great. God is good. Let us thank him for our food. By his hands, we all are fed. Give us, Lord, our daily bread. Amen."

"Now I lay me down to sleep, I pray the Lord my soul to keep. If I should die before I wake, I pray the Lord my soul to take. Amen."

"God in heaven hear my prayer; keep me in thy loving care. Be my guide in all I do. Bless all those who love me too. Amen."

One of the simplest things to do is pray. Yet prayer is also one of the hardest things to do consistently. It's easy to repeat a child's prayer, especially when the prayer rhymes, but it is much harder to pray and feel like you have really touched the heart of God.

Developing a consistent prayer life is essential to growing your faith. Prayer is simply talking to God and listening to his voice. As we talk about prayer this week, we will first look at Jesus' prayer, and then take the remaining four days to discuss the acronym ACTS (adoration, confession, thanksgiving, supplication).

DAY 1

LUKE 11:1–13

In his short model prayer, Jesus mentioned three relationships that make up our lives and are in need of prayer (vv. 2–6). First is our relationship to him: pray for his will to be done. Second is our relationship to ourselves: pray for needs to be met, sins to be forgiven, and temptations to be avoided. Third is our relationship to others: forgive others as you have been forgiven by God. How much better would the quality of your life be if each day you spent time praying about your relationship with God, yourself, and others?

Jesus then gave two analogies: a friend in need (vv. 5–8) and a father's relationship with his son (vv. 11–12). These comparisons emphasize that when we pray, God listens and desires to do what is best for his children. Sandwiched in between these two analogies is the trilogy of asking, seeking, and knocking (vv. 9–10). When we get our relationships right—seeking God's kingdom, being content with having our basic needs met, asking forgiveness of sins, overcoming temptation, and forgiving others—then when we pray and ask, God will give; when we pray and seek, we will find; and when we pray and knock, God will open the door. What a great promise! What incredible power there is when we pray!

In *Total Quality Life*, you can read about an outline of prayer that follows the acronym ACTS—adoration, confession, thanksgiving, supplication. Over the next four days, we will look at each of these in more detail. We will talk about what each one means and steps to incorporate each item into your prayer life.

QUESTIONS FOR REFLECTION

1. If you could ask Jesus one question, what would it be? Why would you ask that particular question?

2. Why do you think prayer is so hard to do consistently?

PRAYER FOR TODAY

Dear Jesus, teach me to pray. Teach me what it means to live a life of prayer, and show me how living such a life will increase my faith. Forgive me for not having a more consistent prayer life. Help me to seek your kingdom, forgive others, and stay away from temptations. In Jesus' name I pray. Amen.

DAY 2

EXODUS 15:1–21

The A in ACTS stands for adoration. *Total Quality Life* says to "start your prayer by acknowledging how great God is. Recognize that he is all-powerful, all-knowing, good, kind, and loving. Tell him you love him for who he is" (p. 87).

In today's Scripture reading, the Israelites had miraculously crossed the Red Sea on dry ground. The Egyptian soldiers, in pursuit of the Israelites, followed them into the Red Sea and drowned (Ex. 14:23–31). God had delivered the Israelites from their enemies. They were now free. In response to God's deliverance, Moses and Miriam give praise to God.

Notice all the ways Moses and Miriam described God: "highly exalted . . . my strength and my song . . . my salvation . . . a warrior . . . LORD . . . majestic in power . . . greatness of your majesty . . . majestic in holiness, awesome in glory, working wonders . . . unfailing love . . . redeemed . . . power of your arm. . . . The LORD will reign forever and ever" (vv. 1–18). Then, in response to this song, Miriam, and all the women, took tambourines in their hands, danced, and sang, "He is highly exalted" (v. 21).

God Almighty is to be adored because of who he is. He is all-powerful (omnipotent), all-knowing (omniscient), and all-present (omnipresent). He is holy, sovereign, powerful, majestic, glorious, frightful, and dangerous. He is full of love, grace, mercy, compassion, and forgiveness. Out of nothing he created everything, and everything is nothing without him. He is the Alpha and Omega, the beginning and the end, the first and the last, the same yesterday, today, and forever. He is both the breath of life and the bread of life. He is the King of Righteousness, the King of Justice, the King Eternal, the King Immortal, and the King Invisible. He is the King of Kings and Lord of Lords. He is the Only Wise God. He is faithful, immutable, and good. He is the Great I Am.

We do not give God praise and adoration because he needs or wants it, for he is self-existing and self-sufficient. We give God praise and adoration because he deserves it and because doing so reminds us of who he is. In the same way looking out at the ocean or staring up into a starry night reminds you of your insignificance, so adoring God reminds you of his greatness and your smallness. Adoring God puts all of life into proper perspective.

QUESTIONS FOR REFLECTION

1. Why do you think it is so important to start your prayer with adoration to God?

2. Of all the ways Moses and Miriam described God in today's Scripture reading, which speaks most to you right now? Why?

3. In addition to the Scripture reading, today's reading listed a lot of attributes of God. Which two or three really jumped out at you? Why?

PRAYER FOR TODAY

My Father, you are God alone, and for that you deserve all praise and adoration. I praise you for your greatness and goodness. I praise you for your omnipotence, omniscience, and omnipresence. I will love you and adore you all the days of my life. In Jesus' name I pray. Amen.

DAY 3

1 JOHN 1:1–10

One of the results of focusing on the characteristics of God and giving him adoration is that you begin to realize how undeserving you are. This sounds like a bad thing, but it is not because by doing so, you realize how dependent you are on God. The Bible makes it clear that all of us are sinners and the wages of sin is death (Rom. 3:23; 6:23). However, because of God's love, mercy, grace, and compassion, we can confess our sins to him and receive forgiveness.

John's letter focuses on two key themes: our need to understand the basics of Christianity and to demonstrate true Christianity by loving one another. John found the most basic expression of our faith in Jesus Christ, the "Word of life" (v. 1). Jesus actually lived and was "seen" and "touched" (v. 1). He "appeared; we have seen it and testify to it, and we proclaim to you the eternal life" (v. 2). John proclaimed the reality of Jesus so that we can have a personal relationship with God through faith in Christ (v. 3).

John added to this basic message that "God is light; in him there is no darkness at all" (v. 5). John was saying that God is truth, perfection, and holiness; and no person who is not truthful, perfect, or holy, can be in fellowship with God. This is a big problem because none of us are perfectly truthful or holy. Every one of us has sinned. So how can we, who are not light but darkness, have fellowship with God who is light?

We can have fellowship with God because the "blood of Jesus . . . purifies us from all sin" (v. 7), and when "we confess our sins, he is faithful and just and will forgive us our sins and purify us from all unrighteousness" (v. 9). To confess means to admit your wrongdoing and turn away from it. When we do so, God acts to forgive us and transform our lives so that we can have fellowship with him.

Today, focus on confessional prayer. As you pray, be specific. Don't be satisfied with "God, forgive me of my sins." Instead, pray, "God, forgive me for losing my temper and saying unkind things to my spouse" or whatever it is that you need to confess. Once you have identified your sins, consider writing them out. There is something powerful about seeing your specific sins written down that make them concrete. It's painful, but it is also cleansing. As a symbol of God's forgiveness, after you have confessed, take that piece of paper and destroy it. God forgives, and he wants to purify you and cleanse you of all sin.

QUESTIONS FOR REFLECTION

1. How do you think focusing on the characteristics of God opens your eyes to your own sinfulness?

2. How did it make you feel to write out your sins? How did it make you feel to destroy that piece of paper, knowing God has forgiven you?

PRAYER FOR TODAY

Lord, I confess my sins to you. I confess my wrong attitudes and wrong behaviors. I recognize that these things are not character flaws. They are sins and cannot stand before a holy God. Thank you so much for forgiving me of my sins. Transform my life so that I will no longer be a slave to sin. In Jesus' name I pray. Amen.

DAY 4

PSALM 100:1–5

Once a year we celebrate Thanksgiving Day. Many people spend the other 364 days grumbling and complaining. What would our homes, communities, work places, and churches look like if we reversed the trend and spent 364 days giving thanks and only one day grumbling and complaining?

It should be easy to live a life of thanksgiving because we have so much for which to be thankful. Every time we pray, we should remember to give God thanks. Today's Scripture reading is an example of a prayer of thanksgiving.

"Shout for joy" (v. 1). The Psalms were songs sung during worship and Psalm 100 was probably a loud, fast-paced song. By the time worshipers were finished singing it, they may have even been a bit hoarse. Have you ever offered thanks to God at the very top of your lungs? Gladness and true joy should characterize our worship and praise to him (v. 2).

Why should we be so loud and jubilant? Because the "LORD is God. It is he who made us, and we are his . . . people, the sheep of his pasture" (v. 3). Let that truth sink in. Almighty God created you, watches over you, provides for you, and protects you. What a reason to shout and be glad! Because of who God is and what he has done, our lives and worship should be characterized with thanksgiving and praise (v. 4). "For the LORD is good and his love endures forever; his faithfulness continues through all generations" (v. 5).

Shout! Go ahead; I dare you. Break the silence of your surroundings and yell out a thanksgiving to God. If it is early in the morning, wake everyone up with your joy and gladness and tell them how great God is. If you are outside, shout at the top of your lungs and give God thanks. If you are sitting in a coffee house, start laughing and clap your hands.

OK, maybe you didn't really shout out loud. Whether you did or didn't, try to live today in such a way that your life shouts joy, gladness, and thanksgiving. Make it your goal today for at least one person to ask you why you are in such a good mood; and then simply answer, "Because I have so much for which to be thankful."

QUESTIONS FOR REFLECTION

1. How can living a life of thanksgiving increase your total quality life? Why do you think it is easier to grumble and complain instead of giving thanks?

2. Make a list of ten things for which you are thankful. How long did it take you to write out that list? What does this say about how much you have been blessed?

PRAYER FOR TODAY

Dear God, thank you. You have been so good to me—better than I have any reason to expect. All I have comes from you. Saying "thanks" seems so inadequate, but I am so very thankful. I love you. May my life be an expression of thanksgiving today. In Jesus' name I pray. Amen.

DAY 5

1 TIMOTHY 2:1–8

This week we have talked about adoration, confession, and thanksgiving. We have not yet talked about bringing our requests to God, and this is the first thing that so often comes to mind when we think of prayer. While making requests is an important part of prayer, it is not the only thing or even the main thing, because God already knows what you need before you even ask. Still, he asks you to bring your requests to him. That is the supplication part of the ACTS acronym.

When Paul gave Timothy instructions for corporate worship, his first instruction was to pray. Even though Paul mentioned thanksgiving in verse 1, his emphasis on prayer here was praying for one another. Another word for *requests* (v. 1) is *supplications*. The word *intercession* includes the idea of drawing so close to someone that you feel empathy for them. When we intercede for someone in prayer, we feel their sorrow, heartache, or joy.

Paul encouraged us to pray for governmental officials and others in authority that they will have wisdom and discernment, so "that we may live peaceful and quiet lives in all godliness and holiness" (v. 2). Pray that they and others you know will come to a transforming knowledge of and faith in Jesus Christ (vv. 5–7).

Paul closed his instructions on prayer by stating, "I want men everywhere to lift up holy hands in prayer, without anger or disputing" (v. 8). In your own personal life and in the life of the church, you cannot overemphasize the importance of prayer and intercession for other people.

One of the most helpful prayer disciplines is to write your prayers. Take a piece of paper or a journal and write your prayer requests to God. It's easy to pray and then forget to give God thanks when he answers our requests. Begin the habit of keeping a prayer journal, including your requests and notes about when and how God answered each request.

One last thing: Each time you pray, try including all four components discussed this week—adoration, confession, thanksgiving, supplication (ACTS). Then, the next time you are called on to pray in public or before a meal, include all four aspects in that prayer as well. ACTS is not a formula but a tool that will increase the quality of your prayer life. When you develop a meaningful prayer life, you will be surprised at how much your faith grows.

QUESTIONS FOR REFLECTION

1. How has this week's study on prayer changed how you will approach praying in the future?

2. Why do you think the first thing Paul told Timothy about corporate worship was how to pray? What does this say about the importance of prayer?

PRAYER FOR TODAY

Dear Lord, I humbly come to you today, praying you will help me grow in my faith. Once again, I ask that you teach me how to pray. I pray I will become a prayer warrior. Lord, help me to begin the habit of writing my prayers and keeping a list of prayer requests and how you answer those prayers. May my life be characterized by prayer, praise, and thanksgiving. I ask all this in Jesus' name. Amen.

WEEK 3

THANKSGIVING

RECOMMENDED READING

Total Quality Life, chapter 2, pages 26–31; chapter 6, pages 88–91

our attitude determines your altitude."

"You can't control what happens to you, but you can control how you react to what happens to you."

The secret ingredient behind both statements is a lifestyle characterized by gratitude and thanksgiving. If your life is full of gratitude and thanksgiving, you will have the proper attitude and react to situations in a way that is constructive. In other words, your gratitude determines your attitude which impacts your altitude and dictates your reactions.

Living a life of gratitude and thanksgiving will increase your faith in God and your total quality life. Thanksgiving is the topic of this week's study, and our text book will be the book of Psalms.

DAY 1

PSALM 105

It is far easier to see God's hand of providence in the rearview mirror than it is through the windshield. Looking back over your life, seeing how God provided and protected even when you were unaware of it can be a great source of thanksgiving.

Psalm 105 begins with a call to "give thanks to the LORD, call on his name" (v. 1). To call means to make a proclamation or to make God famous. The definition of the word *call* is given in the next phrase, "make [God's name] known among the nations" (v. 1). Giving thanks to God for all he has done is the best witness about who he is.

What are we to give thanks to God about? What are we to say about him to make him famous in the world? The psalmist told us two things about God for which we are to give thanks. First, we are to give thanks to God for the "wonders he has done" (v. 5). We are to look back and remember "his miracles, and the judgments he pronounced" (v. 5). When you look back over your life, can you point to times where you know God acted and intervened on your behalf or on behalf of your family? Remember those times and give thanks.

Second, the psalmist encourages us to give thanks for God's faithfulness. This is the subject of the rest of the psalm, but it begins in verse 8 with these words: God "remembers his covenant forever." Psalms 105 and 106 go together. (We will look at Ps. 106 tomorrow.) These two psalms were written either by David or by his song director, Asaph, when the ark of the covenant was brought back to Jerusalem (see 2 Sam. 6:12–19; 1 Chron. 16:1–7). The ark of the covenant represented God's relationship with his people. By bringing the ark back from their enemies into Jerusalem, God was proving himself faithful. The nation had gone through a difficult time, but God was, and still is, faithful. He will do what he promised. The rest of the psalm is a review of how God has faithfully protected, provided for, and delivered his people.

Are you going through a tough time? Does it seem like God has abandoned you? Don't give up! Remember what God has done in the past and know that he is faithful. Right now you may not see it. But one day, looking back, you will see how God protected and provided for you, even when you were unaware of his presence.

Give thanks.

QUESTIONS FOR REFLECTION

1. How can you make God known to other people by giving thanks?

2. What are some of the wonders of God you have seen? How can you thank God for those wonders?

3. In what ways has God proven himself faithful to you? What times in your life has God protected, provided for, and delivered you?

PRAYER FOR TODAY

Lord, thank you for your wonders and faithfulness. At times, I have doubted you, but every time, you prove yourself to be faithful and true. Thank you for all the ways you have protected and provided for me and my family. Thank you for all the ways you have delivered us. In Jesus' name I pray. Amen.

DAY 2

PSALM 106

In the heat of the battle of everyday life, it is often hard to see God at work and give thanks. It sometimes takes reflecting on the past, instead of dwelling on the present, to see the hand of God at work. When we reflect on the past and give thanks, we receive hope for the present and strength to move into the future.

The ark of the covenant, which represented God's presence and his personal relationship with Israel (2 Sam. 6), had been in the hands of Israel's enemies for one hundred years. After recapturing Jerusalem and with thirty thousand warriors at his side, King David set his sights on retrieving the ark and bringing it home (2 Sam. 6). At times, it might have seemed that God left his people, but each time it was the people who had abandoned him. The return of the ark to Jerusalem signified a return to God, and it was a reason to celebrate and give thanks. Psalm 106 was written at the time the ark was brought back to Jerusalem.

The psalmist began by encouraging the reader to praise the Lord and give thanks because "he is good" (v. 1). There may be more lofty ways to describe God, but there is no greater truth than to simply say God is good. Wherever there is goodness in the world, it is because God is good, and his presence is everywhere. The primary manifestation of God's goodness is his love that "endures forever" (v. 1). And the main way we see his enduring love is in his willingness to forgive our sins.

The psalmist said, "We have sinned, even as our fathers did; we have done wrong and acted wickedly" (v. 6). The writer then listed the sins of the Israelites throughout their history. In Egypt, they gave no thought to God and even rebelled while he was delivering them from bondage (v. 7). Yet, in spite of their sins, God rescued them (vv. 8–10). As a result, the people "believed his promises and sang his praise" (v. 12).

But then the people sinned by forgetting God and becoming envious of Moses and Aaron. So God sent "a severe plague" (Num. 11:33) and an earthquake that killed thousands (Num. 16). They worshiped idols, despised God's gifts, grumbled and complained, and did many other things that angered the Lord (Ps. 106:16–46). Still, the people eventually cried out to God to save them (v. 47), and God forgave and rescued them. "Praise be to the LORD, the God of Israel, from everlasting to everlasting. Let all the people say, 'Amen!' Praise the LORD" (v. 48).

If it were not for God's goodness and everlasting love, we would be doomed. But he is good; his love lasts forever; and he has cleansed our sins. Give thanks to God and praise his name.

QUESTIONS FOR REFLECTION

1. Over the last two days, five reasons have been given to thank God: (1) his wonders, (2) his faithfulness, (3) his goodness, (4) his everlasting love, and (5) his forgiveness. Which of the five reasons mean the most to you? Why?

2. In what ways can you give thanks to God today for his forgiveness of sins?

PRAYER FOR TODAY

Lord, thank you for your goodness and everlasting love. Without your mercy and grace, I would have no reason for hope, now or in the future. Help me to never forget your kindness in my life. In Jesus' name I pray. Amen.

DAY 3

PSALM 107

Have you felt abandoned by God? Have you gone through a time when giving thanks was the furthest thing from your mind? What do you do when you feel like an exile? What do you do when you can't give thanks? In today's Scripture reading, we learn in such times to focus on God's love by reminding ourselves that his love is unfailing. God loves you even when you can't feel his presence. God loves you even when you doubt his existence. God loves you even when you don't feel that he does, and he loves you even when you are angry at him.

Psalm 107 was probably written while the Israelites where exiled in Babylon, or right after they were delivered from the exile. It is a call for the redeemed (v. 2) to give thanks. To be redeemed means to be delivered. The Israelites had been delivered from the exile, and those who place their faith in Jesus have been delivered from their sins. The theme of this psalm is to give thanks because God's unfailing love has delivered you from your distress.

The psalm contains four cycles. In each cycle, the people find themselves in trouble because they have turned their backs on God. During their trouble, "they cried out to the LORD . . . and he delivered them from their distress" (v. 6; see vv. 13, 19, 28). As a result of God's deliverance, the psalm exhorts, "Let them give thanks to the LORD for his unfailing love and his wonderful deeds for men" (vv. 8, 15, 21; see v. 43). Each time, examples are given of God's wonderful deeds.

Sometimes, Christians fall into a similar cycle of disobedience, rebellion, repentance, and deliverance. But this is not the Christian life God intended. God sent his Son so that we could have victory over sin, and for that, we can be thankful. The apostle Paul said, "But God demonstrated his own love for us in this: While we were still sinners, Christ died for us. . . . For I am convinced that neither death nor life, neither angels nor demons, neither the present nor the future, nor any powers, neither height nor depth, nor anything else in all creation, will be able to separate us from the love of God that is in Christ Jesus our Lord" (Rom. 5:8; 8:38–39).

Let those who have been redeemed by God give thanks for his deliverance! Are you part of the redeemed?

QUESTIONS FOR REFLECTION

1. Has there been a time in your life when you felt abandoned and alone? What happened? How did you come out of those feelings?

2. How can you know God loves you, even when he feels far away and when you don't feel like he loves you?

3. How does the cycle mentioned in Psalm 107 describe certain times in your life? How have you experienced deliverance from the cycle itself?

PRAYER FOR TODAY

Dear God, thank you for delivering me from my sins and distress. Thank you for your unfailing love. Thank you for loving me, even when I feel distanced from you, and even when I wonder how anyone could love me. Thank you. In Jesus' name I pray. Amen.

DAY 4

PSALM 118:1–29

A well-known politician hosted a fundraising dinner. The dinner was limited to a certain number of people, and the price to attend was high. Those who attended the dinner were invited to meet and greet the politician at no extra charge. All they had to do was to pick up a separate ticket for this. The free ticket provided entrance into the small room to meet the VIP.

Through his death and resurrection, Jesus Christ paid the price for your seat at the great banquet table. Dinner will not be served until Christ returns, but while you wait for dinner, you are invited to a meet and greet at no extra charge. The ticket for this event is to give thanks.

In verses 19–20 of today's Scripture, the psalmist waited for the gates of heaven to be opened so he could meet the Lord. What opened the gate was to "give thanks to the LORD." Psalm 118 begins and ends with a call to give thanks (vv. 1, 29). Sandwiched in the middle is this idea that thanksgiving opens the gates to the Lord.

In this psalm, the writer mentioned eight things about God for which we should be thankful: the Lord is our helper who will ensure victory over our enemies (v. 7); our refuge (vv. 8–9); our deliverer (vv. 10–12); our strength (v. 14); our song or source of joy (v. 14); our salvation (v. 14); and the source of eternal life (v. 17). The last thing the psalmist mentioned for which we can be thankful is that the Lord is our discipliner (v. 18). For those who have placed their faith in Jesus Christ, God doesn't punish us; rather, he disciplines us. It may sound strange, but we can be thankful for this, even when his discipline is severe, because we know his discipline comes out of his love for us.

It is precisely because we have so much for which to be thankful that the writer said, "This is the day the LORD has made; let us rejoice and be glad in it" (v. 24). Living a life characterized by gratitude and thankfulness makes every day a good day. "You are my God, and I will give you thanks; you are my God, and I will exalt you" (v. 28).

QUESTIONS FOR REFLECTION

1. What do you think it means to say that giving thanks is the ticket (or key) that opens the gates to the Lord?

2. Of the eight things the psalmist said we can be thankful for, which one means the most to you? Why?

PRAYER FOR TODAY

Dear God, I am overwhelmed with thanksgiving to you and for you. You are a great God. Today, I am most thankful for Jesus. You are indeed my salvation and the source of my eternal life. Through your strength and help, I will be victorious. In Jesus' name I pray. Amen.

DAY 5

Psalm 136

Twenty-six times the psalmist wrote, "*His love endures forever.*" The Hebrew word for *love* is *chesed*. In addition to love, it can also be translated as *goodness*, *kindness*, *devotion*, *faithfulness*, *mercy*, *loving-kindness*, or *unchanging love*. Thus, the writer of Psalm 136 is telling us that God will never change; he will always be loving, kind, merciful, faithful, good, devoted, and unchanging.

Psalm 136 was written to be sung as a call and response. The song director would sing the first line of every verse and the people would respond, "*His love endures forever.*" Woven throughout the passage is a brief history of the world through the eyes of God's people, Israel. The story starts with creation (vv. 4–9) and continues through Israel's deliverance from their bondage in Egypt, desert wanderings, entrance into the Promised Land, and God's continual provision for them (vv. 10–25). By the end of the psalm, you can imagine that the whole congregation is on their feet clapping, crying, shouting, "Give thanks to the God of heaven. His love endures forever" (v. 26).

Stop and think about your story. Reflect on your life. Think about all the ups and downs, good and bad. Remember those times when God protected, provided for, and delivered you. Through all the things that have happened, are happening now, and will happen in the future, the one thing you can count on is that God is the same. He does not change. His love and mercy will endure forever and even beyond. Because of who God is and because of what he has done, you can be thankful and move confidently into the future. Praise his holy name!

QUESTIONS FOR REFLECTION

1. What do you think it means to say that God's love will endure forever? What kind of hope would that truth give to people who are struggling?

2. How can remembering your story help you be thankful for all God has done for you?

3. What can you begin doing this week to help develop a lifestyle of gratitude and thanksgiving?

PRAYER FOR TODAY

Father, what a great week it has been! I am humbled by your enduring love and everlasting mercy. I am encouraged by how you have always been with me. I now move confidently into the future. I pray you will help me to continue to be a person who is grateful and thankful for all things. I pray all this in Jesus' name. Amen.

WEEK 4

MEDITATION

RECOMMENDED READING

Total Quality Life, chapter 6, pages 91–96

Have you ever done something without thinking? Have you ever spoken without thinking? As a teenager, did you ever get in trouble and have your parents frustratingly ask, "What were you thinking?" Has the outcome of acting without thinking ever been positive?

Proverbs 23:7 states, "For as he thinks in his heart, so *is* he" (NKJV). In other words, what a person dwells on—what one meditates on—defines that person. The origin of our outward actions is our inward thoughts. The simple truth is that we never do anything without first thinking. Thus, meditating on right things is extremely important, and the best you can meditate on is God. The words *think* and *thank* are closely related. So, to think about God is one way we can give thanks to him.

Meditation, thinking about God, is a powerful way to grow in your faith and increase your total quality life. Meditation is also our topic of study this week. During this week, at the end of each day, you will be given suggested steps for meditation.

DAY 1

PSALM 19:1–14

To meditate means to muse over, ponder, reflect upon, and think about. Meditation is a focused concentration on a particular thought. Unfortunately, many people today associate the word *meditation* with various non-Christian philosophies and practices. However, the practice of meditation is firmly rooted in both the Old and New Testaments, even if it has become somewhat of a lost art in modern Christianity.

Two Hebrew words in the Old Testament are translated *meditation*. One is *haga*, which means to utter, groan, or ponder. The other is *sihach*, which means to muse, contemplate, reflect, or rehearse in one's mind. In today's Scripture reading, a form of the word *haga* is used.

Today's passage divides easily into two parts. The focus of part one (vv. 1–6) is God's created world, and the focus of part two (vv. 7–14) is God's revealed Word.

All creation declares God's glory, making him known. No language more articulately speaks forth God's majesty and wonder than the imagery of his creation. Every moment, God's created world testifies to his power, and the most powerful part of God's creation is the sun. Sun worship was widespread in ancient civilizations, but David (the composer of Psalm 19) pictured the sun as part of God's creation. Instead of worshiping the sun, David wrote, "[God] has pitched a tent for the sun" (v. 4).

While God's created world speaks to his glory and power, his revealed Word speaks to his care and concern for you and me. "The law of the LORD . . . the statutes of the LORD . . . the precepts of the

LORD . . . the commands of the LORD . . . the fear of the LORD . . . the ordinances of the LORD" (vv. 7–9) tell us all we need to know about God and what he requires of us. God's revealed Word is trustworthy, right, radiant, pure, and sure. Through his Word "is [his] servant warned; in keeping them there is great reward" (v. 11). In response to God's world and Word, David concluded, "May the words of my mouth and the meditation of my heart be pleasing in your sight, O LORD, my Rock and my Redeemer" (v. 14).

STEPS FOR MEDITATION

Scripture memorization: Being able to recite Scripture from memory is a wonderful way to meditate on God's Word. During this week, memorize Psalm 119:14.

Scripture prayer: Closely related to memorizing Scripture is choosing a phrase in the Bible and repeating it as a form of prayer throughout your day. Phrases like "The LORD is my Shepherd" (Ps. 23:1), "We live by faith" (2 Cor. 5:7), and "The joy of the LORD is [my] strength" (Neh. 8:10) will keep you focused throughout the day on the things of God. Some possible prayers from today's Scripture reading could be "The heavens declare the glory of God" (Ps. 19:1), "The law of the LORD is perfect" (v. 7), or "The fear of the LORD is pure" (v. 9).

QUESTIONS FOR REFLECTION

1. Take a few moments to meditate on the beauty of God's created world. As you meditate, what are some of the things that come to your mind about God?

2. Take a few moments to meditate on the gift of God's revealed Word. As you meditate, what are some of the things that come to your mind about God?

PRAYER FOR TODAY

Dear God, I praise you for who you are. I love you, and I want my life to be a reflection and proclamation of your glory. Your power is seen in creation, and your personality is reflected in your Word. Both are wonderful gifts and worthy of my meditation. Dear God, teach me what it means to meditate on you. In Jesus' name. Amen.

DAY 2

JOHN 15:1–8

Have you ever been so deep in thought about something that you completely blocked out everything going on around you? Have you ever been so deep in thought about something that someone had to shake you or snap their fingers in your face and say, "Snap out of it"? If you have done either of those things, then you already know how to meditate. Meditation is a laser like focus on something. Chances are that you have had such focus on your job, hobby, or something that is concerning you. But have you ever been so deep in thought about the things of God that you have been oblivious to what was taking place around you?

In today's Scripture reading, Jesus tells us that remaining in him—staying focused and meditating on him—is the key to growing in our faith.

The purpose of a vine is to bear fruit, and when a vine does not bear fruit, it is cut off by the gardener. Vines that do bear fruit are pruned so they can produce even more fruit (v. 2). What's the difference between being cut off and being pruned? Pruning is cutting back the ends of the vine so that it can grow stronger, whereas cutting off involves removing branches from the vine, their very source of life. The only way a branch can bear fruit is by remaining in the vine. Likewise, the only way a believer can be fruitful is by remaining in Jesus.

The Greek word translated *remain* (vv. 4–7) is *meno*, and means to stay or abide. Jesus says to abide in him, and he will abide in us. As we abide in him, we will be fruitful and productive. In fact, Jesus said, "Apart from me you can do nothing" (v. 5).

One way we abide in Jesus is to meditate on his teachings: "If you remain in me and my words remain in you . . ." (v. 7). As we meditate and focus on Jesus' teachings, our desires and wants become his desires and wants so that we can "ask whatever [we] wish, and it will be given to [us]" (v. 7). What an incredible promise! Not only is this a promise, but it is also the very purpose for what it means to be Jesus' disciple (v. 8).

STEPS FOR MEDITATION

Contemplative prayer: Select a short Scripture or biblical passage, write it down, and reflect on it for an entire day. Think about how the Scripture relates to your life. Take ownership of the Scripture by asking God to show you how you need to apply what you are hearing from him.

Topical singing: Most church song books have a topical concordance in them. Look up a particular topic in the song book—grace, mercy, salvation, love, etc.—and sing or recite out loud the songs that deal with the topic you have chosen for the day.

QUESTIONS FOR REFLECTION

1. What do you think it means to abide in Jesus? How can you remain in him throughout your everyday life?

2. What do you think Jesus meant when he said, "If you remain in me and my words remain in you, ask whatever you wish, and it will be given to you" (v. 7)?

PRAYER FOR TODAY

Dear Jesus, help me learn what it means to remain in you. Lord, teach me to abide in you in all situations. My desire is to be fruitful and productive for you and your kingdom. Show me how to meditate on you. I love you. In Jesus' name. Amen.

DAY 3

PSALM 119:9–16

Meditation is hard work. At the precise moment you try to block out everything and focus on God, you may remember where you placed that lost item, all the things you have to do will come flooding to your mind, or you will start to think of all the items you need at the grocery store. It takes focus to sit and be still and meditate on the things of God. It can help to have a blank piece of paper and pen with you when you meditate so you can write down all the things that come to your mind and get them out of the way so you can focus on God.

Psalm 119 is the longest psalm and chapter in the Bible. Each of the twenty-two sections of the psalm has eight lines, and the first line in each section starts with the corresponding Hebrew letter. The entire psalm is about the importance of Holy Scripture. The psalmist referred to God's Word in eight ways: law, testimonies, precepts, statutes, commandments, judgments, word, and ordinances. Today's passage is eight lines, beginning with the second letter of the Hebrew alphabet, and Holy Scripture is described as God's Word.

The psalmist wrote that it is through God's Word that we stay pure (v. 9). To be pure means to be clean or blameless. The way you live by God's Word is by seeking it with all your heart, obeying every command, and hiding God's Word in your heart (vv. 10–11). The idea behind hiding God's Word in your heart is to treat it as something to be valued and protected at all costs. It means to make God's Word of primary importance in your life. The idea is to continually meditate on God's Word. The psalmist wrote, "I meditate on your precepts and consider your ways. I delight in your decrees; I will not neglect your word" (vv. 15–16).

There is no more powerful antidote to sin in your life than meditating on the Word of God.

STEPS FOR MEDITATION

Journaling: Begin a spiritual journal to record your thoughts about God, what you are reading in his Word, and what you are hearing from him. As you meditate on him, write down what comes to your mind.

Prayer walking: As you walk around your neighborhood, pray and ask God to show you how best to pray for your neighbors. Ask God to show you how best to build relationships with those in your neighborhood who are far from him.

QUESTIONS FOR REFLECTION

1. What do you think it means to sin against God (v. 11)? What do you think it means to hide God's Word in your heart (v. 11)?

2. How do you think hiding God's Word in your heart keeps you from sinning against God?

PRAYER FOR TODAY

Dear God, I want to live a pure life and a life that is pleasing to you. I pray you will give me the power to do so. I also confess that the power to live such a life comes from meditating on your Word. I pray that as I meditate on your Word, you will lead and guide me. In Jesus' name I pray. Amen.

DAY 4

PSALM 139:1–24

In any relationship, communication is a two-way street. If one person does all the talking, it's not an intimate relationship. In your relationship with God, if you do all the talking, then the relationship is out of balance. God never speaks contrary to his Word, but he can and does speak directly to us in a more intimate, personal way through meditation. It is through reading and meditating on God's Word that we learn his will for our lives and receive direction for our next step.

Psalm 139 is made up of four stanzas with six verses each. The first three stanzas are meditations on God's omniscience, omnipresence, and omnipotence. The last stanza is David's response to the majesty of God found in the first three stanzas.

David confessed that Almighty God knows every move you make before you make them. He knows your thoughts (v. 2) and words before you speak them (v. 4). David said, "Such knowledge is too wonderful for me, too lofty for me to attain" (v. 6). Meditate on the fact that God is omniscient. He knows everything about you. He knows the good and the bad. He knows these things and he still loves you.

Not only does God know everything, God is also everywhere at the same time. David said there was nowhere he could go that God wasn't already there. He could have gone to the outermost part of the universe and the deepest depth of the sea, and God would be there (vv. 7–8). The analogies "wings of the dawn" and "far side of the sea" (v. 9) express great distance. David could have gone as far east and as far west as a person can travel, and God would still be there guiding him (v. 10). Even darkness does not hide you from God's presence (vv. 11–12). Meditate on the fact that God is omnipresent. He is everywhere at the same time and at all times.

The power of God is best seen in creation, and his greatest creation is you. He created your "inmost being" and he "knit [you] together in [your] mother's womb" (v. 13). No wonder David praised God: "I am fearfully and wonderfully made" (v. 14). God watched over your creation from conception through birth, and he has your days planned out (vv. 15–16). Meditate on the fact that God is omnipotent. He is all-powerful and created you for a purpose.

In response to God's omniscience, omnipresence, and omnipotence, David cried out for God to continue to watch over him, keep him safe from his enemies, and keep him from sin (vv. 19–22). The proper response to Almighty God, for any of us, is to pray, "Search me, O God, and know my heart; test me and know my anxious thoughts. See if there is any offensive way in me, and lead me in the way everlasting" (vv. 23–24).

STEPS FOR MEDITATION

Focused concentration: Write on an index card, "God is omniscient." Write on another card, "God is omnipresent;" and on a third card, "God is omnipotent." Spend five to ten minutes looking at each cards and meditating on what each phrase means. On the cards, write all that comes to your mind as you are meditating.

Psalm writing: Write your own psalm (or song or poem). Choose a characteristic of God to focus on and write about it. End the psalm by writing your response to that particular characteristic of God.

QUESTIONS FOR REFLECTION

1. What does it mean to you to say that God is omniscient? How would you describe his omniscience to someone else?

2. What does it mean to you to say that God is omnipresent? How would you describe his omnipresence to someone else?

3. What does it mean to you to say that God is omnipotent? How would you describe his omnipotence to someone else?

PRAYER FOR TODAY

God, I praise and thank you for your omniscience, omnipresence, and omnipotence. Knowing you are all-knowing, all-present, and all-powerful, encourages me and gives me confidence to move into your future. It also challenges and motivates me to live a life that is pleasing to you. I love you. In Jesus' name. Amen.

DAY 5

PSALM 77:1–20

It doesn't matter if you had good reasons or not, and it doesn't matter if you are angry and disillusioned with other people, life, or God. When you feel yourself losing control, it is always good advice to take time to calm down. According to today's Scripture reading, taking time to meditate on God is a good way to calm down and regain your senses when things seem out of control.

The psalmist Asaph was angry and disillusioned. He began his psalm by crying out to God for help in his distress (vv. 1–2). The Hebrew word translated *distress* (*tsarah*) could be translated as anguish, affliction, or trouble. Asaph didn't tell us what the trouble is, but he did say that it had been keeping him up at night, "and [his] soul refused to be comforted" (v. 2).

Asaph then peppered God (or anyone who would listen) with six questions (vv. 7–9): Will God reject me? Will God never be pleased with me again? Is God's love gone forever? Do God's promises mean nothing? Has God forgotten how to be merciful? And has God's anger overshadowed his compassion? Have you ever wanted to yell at God, and ask questions like these? Most of us do at some point in our lives.

Asaph said that in the middle of his anger and disillusionment, he was reminded of the "deeds of the LORD" and remembered the miracles God had performed in the past (v. 11). He then retold the story of how God delivered the Israelites from Egyptian bondage (vv. 13–20).

Asaph said that the way to calm down when we are angry and disillusioned is by meditating on all God's works and considering all his mighty deeds (v. 12). No matter what you are going through and no matter how angry you have become, the best way to calm down when things seem out of control is to meditate on God, focusing on how he has provided for and protected his people. He is the same yesterday, today, and forever. He has not forgotten you. He still loves you. His promises are true, and his mercy and compassion last forever.

STEPS FOR MEDITATION

An ancient form of Christian meditation is called *lectio divina*, meaning "sacred reading." Lectio divina has four stages: (1) reading (*lectio*)—read a passage of Scripture slowly and deliberately; (2) meditation (*meditatio*)—reflect on the passage; (3) prayer (*oratio*)—pray the passage back to God, asking the Holy Spirit to reveal truth; and (4) contemplation (*contemplatio*)—think about the implication of what you have read and the truth that has been revealed.

QUESTIONS FOR REFLECTION

1. Look at the six questions the psalmist asked. How many have you asked before? Can you think of similar questions you have asked?

2. How do you think meditating on what God has done in the past will help you deal with the present and prepare for the future?

PRAYER FOR TODAY

Lord God, thank you for this week and the emphasis on meditating on you. I pray you will continue to challenge and teach me to be still and quiet before you. Help me to slow down long enough for you to speak to me. Thank you for your compassion and mercy. In Jesus' name I pray. Amen.

WEEK 5

FELLOWSHIP

RECOMMENDED READING

Total Quality Life, chapter 8, pages 136–139

Are zebras white animals with black stripes or black animals with white stripes? I don't know, but what I do know is that somehow the stripes on a zebra serve as camouflage in the wild. On a hot African plain, when a predator sees a herd of zebras from a distance, the zebras' stripes produce the illusion of heat waves. In a herd, a zebra's stripes make him invisible. But a zebra standing alone sticks out like a . . . zebra with stripes.

A zebra's life depends on sticking close to other zebras. Likewise for Christians, there is protection in community. And you need protection, because "your enemy the devil prowls around like a roaring lion looking for someone to devour" (1 Pet. 5:8). Living a total quality life means maintaining close fellowship with other believers.

DAY 1

JOHN 17:20–26

Fellowship and prayer go together. While Jesus' most famous prayer is the Lord's Prayer (Matt. 6:9–15), his most important prayer may have been the one he prayed in the garden of Gethsemane on the night he was arrested. The theme of his prayer was unity among believers based on the unity between God the Father and God the Son. The prayer is found in John 17. In today's Scripture, we will look at the conclusion of that prayer.

In the first part of the prayer, Jesus prays specifically for his disciples (vv. 1–19). After he prays for them, he turns his attention to you and me. Consider that for a moment: On the night he was betrayed and arrested, Jesus was thinking of and praying for you. How do I know he was praying for you? Because he said he was praying for all "who will believe in me through [the disciples'] message" (v. 20). If you believe in Jesus, it is because the disciples did their job of getting the message to the world.

Jesus' prayer for us is that we would be united with the same type of fellowship Jesus had with the Father. Jesus wanted us to have fellowship because our unity shows the world he is God's Son (vv. 21–23). Few things are more important for our testimony to the world than living in love, unity, and fellowship with one another.

In his prayer, Jesus gave two reasons why unity and fellowship are important for his followers. First, unity and fellowship are the essence of the church. Followers of Jesus have been called to live a life that is counter to how the world lives, and a characteristic of that difference is our unity and fellowship. A good word that describes both unity and fellowship is *community*. If we both profess Jesus as Lord, then we have a *common-unity*.

Second, unity and fellowship are also essential for evangelism. True community will draw others to Jesus and the church. Disunity repels people from Jesus and the church. Unity and fellowship are vital for our reputation in the world. Nothing hurts the testimony of Jesus and his church more than believers refusing to live in community with one another.

Are you living in unity and fellowship with other believers? Are you the answer to Jesus' prayer?

QUESTIONS FOR REFLECTION

1. How important is it for believers to live in fellowship with other believers? Why do you think some are reluctant to be involved in the life and fellowship of a church?

2. How does it make you feel to realize that on the night he was betrayed and arrested, Jesus was praying for you?

3. Which of the two reasons given for the importance of unity and fellowship is the most important? Why?

PRAYER FOR TODAY

Dear Jesus, I am moved by the thought that you were thinking of me on the most difficult night of your life. I pray I will be an answer to your prayer and strive to live in unity and fellowship with other believers. Thank you for showing me the importance of living in fellowship with others. In your name I pray. Amen.

DAY 2

1 PETER 3:8–22

Life is not fair. Bad things happen to good people, and good things happen to bad people. There is injustice all around, and if you think about it too long, it can get discouraging. Sometimes the unfairness and injustice is directed at you because of your faith. All around the world and all through history, believers have suffered for their faith. When bad things happen, and when persecution occurs, the one thing that will keep you going is your fellowship with other believers. Without the prayers, support, and encouragement of your fellow Christians, you are more susceptible to the attack of the Enemy.

Today's passage begins, "Finally, all of you, live in harmony with one another" (v. 8). In the previous verses, Peter had addressed specific people in the church (leaders, husbands, wives, etc.); now he was addressing the entire congregation, and his main exhortation was to "live in harmony with one another" (v. 8). The word *harmony* means like-minded. The idea is to be agreeable, thinking the same things, maintaining unity in the church. Peter then listed five things we can do to maintain harmony: be sympathetic; love each other; be compassionate; be humble; and don't repay wrong with more wrong (vv. 8–9).

Following God and pursuing harmony is not always an easy way to live, and it can sometimes make life more difficult. Peter said it is a blessing to suffer for doing what is right (v. 14). Instead of running from suffering, we should embrace it, making Jesus Lord, and be ready to explain to others how we can have such joy in the midst of troubles (vv. 15–16). Jesus is our model for living such a life (vv. 18–22).

If you were to place a bunch of grapes in a plastic bag, the grapes would be together, but they would not have unity. However, if you applied pressure to the bag, crushing the grapes, they would begin to merge into one another to the point when you would no longer be able to distinguish one from the other. In fact, they would no longer be grapes, but grape juice. As we live in community with others, we will walk through the good and bad. But the pressures of life should press us into each other more, creating something sweet and beautiful. Becoming something together that we could never be on our own is the essence of the fellowship and community Jesus wants us to have. But it only happens under pressure.

QUESTIONS FOR REFLECTION

1. Peter listed five things you could do to maintain harmony in the church. Which one of the five do you think is the most important? Why?

2. As believers, why do you think it is important to embrace suffering instead of running from suffering? What role does the church play in helping you deal with suffering?

PRAYER FOR TODAY

Dear God, I praise and thank you for the community of believers to which I belong. I have not always appreciated your church, but I am learning how important it is to walk in harmony with other believers. Life is difficult. Thank you for not requiring me to walk through life alone. In Jesus' name I pray. Amen.

DAY 3

PHILIPPIANS 2:1–11

There is an old saying that goes, "Two chickens tied at the legs and thrown over a clothesline may be united, but they don't have unity." As a believer, it is important that you unite yourself with a local church, but unity means far more than simply showing up in a building each week. True unity goes much deeper.

The church is to display unity because, in Christ, we have shared in the experience of five things: encouragement, comfort, fellowship, tenderness, and compassion. Because of our shared experience in Christ and because we have received such wonderful gifts from him, we should be "like-minded" (v. 2). In what ways are we to be like-minded? Paul explained that it involves "having the same love, being one in spirit and purpose" (v. 2).

We are to love each other the way Christ loved us—unconditionally, sacrificially, and persistently. The phrase "one in spirit" (v. 2) is one word in the Greek, meaning "together in soul." In Christ and because of Christ, we are to treat each other as soul mates. In this verse, Paul is emphatically saying to the believers in Philippi and to us, "Be united!" Since you are one in Christ, be one with each other.

Unity will unlock the door to your church's potential. Unity is your testimony to the world that you are indeed Christians. Together in Christ, there is nothing your church cannot do. There is no challenge your church cannot face. There is no obstacle your church cannot overcome. A united church is a powerful church. A united church shows the world what it means to be an authentic Christian. Unity doesn't mean uniformity, but it does mean working together for the glory of God.

It is impossible to have unity and fellowship in the church without humility. Far from being a sign of weakness, humility is a sign of strength. It demonstrates total contentment and complete trust in God.

Humility unlocks the door to your potential in Jesus Christ, and that potential is limited only by God's plans for you, which are great. As followers of Jesus, you are to regard fellow believers as being above you, and therefore rightful objects of service.

In verses 5–11, Paul recited an early church hymn that the Philippians may have been familiar with. This hymn embodies the essence of Christian faith. Through humility Jesus fulfilled his potential. Likewise, as you humble yourself, God will use your life to make a significant difference.

QUESTIONS FOR REFLECTION

1. In what ways do you think unity would unlock the potential of your church?

2. In what ways to you think humility would unlock the potential in your life?

3. What would happen in your family and church if everyone lived by Philippians 2:3?

PRAYER FOR TODAY

Dear God, thank you for showing me the importance of unity and fellowship in my church. I pray for the strength, wisdom, and humility as you give me opportunities to lead my church in true unity and fellowship. In Jesus' name I pray. Amen.

DAY 4

GALATIANS 6:1–10

Saint Augustine once said, "He who does not have the church as his mother does not have God as his Father." The church is extremely important to your life of faith, and not being a part of the church can be detrimental to your spiritual development. In today's Scripture reading, Paul gave five benefits of being involved in church. Each benefit enhances your quality of faith.

The first benefit of being involved in a church is accountability. When you surround yourself with loving Christians, they will hold you accountable and lovingly "restore" you when you get off track (v. 1). The Greek word translated *restore* (*katartizete*) was used to describe setting a broken bone. Holding yourself and others accountable is painful but necessary for healing to take place.

A second benefit of being involved in a church is assistance. Paul wrote, "Carry each other's burdens" (v. 2). God never intended you to walk through life alone, and he never intended you to carry all of your troubles by yourself. We are taught to be strong, put up walls, and not let others see our weaknesses, but God knows we need brothers and sisters in Christ to assist us in carrying our burdens. But for this to happen, we have to humble ourselves and let others know we are troubled. We also need to pray for discernment so we will know when others need our help.

Encouragement is the third benefit of being involved in a church. In verse 5, Paul encouraged us to carry our own load. This does not contradict what he said before. The burdens referred to in verse 1 are the heavy loads that no person can carry by themselves. The Greek word translated *load* in verse 5 means portion (*phortion*) and pictures the backpack individual soldiers were required to carry. Jesus has given each of us responsibilities, and it is in living in fellowship with other believers that we receive the encouragement needed to fulfill those responsibilities.

A fourth benefit of belonging to a church is instruction. Those who are responsible for teaching us should be adequately compensated (v. 6).

The final benefit is opportunity to do good. It's not easy to do good. At times we will be tempted to quit. But Paul reminded us that we will reap what we sow and we will be rewarded for not giving up (vv. 7–9).

QUESTIONS FOR REFLECTION

1. Read the above quote by St. Augustine again. What do you think he meant? Do you agree with what he said? Why or why not?

2. Of the five benefits to being involved in a church that were given in today's reading, which do you think is the most important? Why?

3. Why do you think Paul said we should do good to all people but then added, "especially to those who belong to the family of believers" (v. 10)? What do you think he meant?

PRAYER FOR TODAY

Dear Lord, I know you are my Father, and I embrace the church as my spiritual mother. Thank you for parenting me. Thank you for giving me a place where I can be held accountable, given assistance, encouraged, instructed, and have opportunities to serve. I love your church, Lord. In Jesus' name I pray. Amen.

DAY 5

1 CORINTHIANS 1:10–17

No church is perfect because no perfect people attend church. Divisions have always been a problem among God's people. The root of most church problems is people insisting on having their own way. However, a divided church is a contradiction of terms.

Paul pleaded with the believers in Corinth to "agree with one another so that there may be no divisions among you" (v. 10). The word translated *divisions* (*schisma*) is where we get our English word *schism*. The word means to split. There should be no open breaks or fractures in the church. Instead, the church should be "perfectly united" (v. 10). The word translated "perfectly united" is a medical term used to describe the setting of a fractured bone, to mend and restore it.

Do you see the picture Paul was painting? The church is the body of Christ, and divisions in the church are like broken bones. Paul wanted the church to mend and restore its broken bones. There were arguments in the church at Corinth that led to people taking sides (vv. 11–12). Have you ever been caught in the middle of a disagreement between two friends? If you have, then you know if you take one person's side, you will make the other person mad, and if you take no sides, you will make them both mad.

When Christians get in arguments, it is usually because they have lost focus on what is really important. Verse 13 serves as a reality check to bring people back to their senses. Paul wrote, "Is Christ divided? Was Paul crucified for you? Were you baptized into the name of Paul?" (v. 13). The answers to these questions are obvious. The people at Corinth were starting to follow the people preaching Christ, instead of following Jesus. The more they focused on personalities, the more they lost sight of the big picture that Jesus died for them, baptized them, and forgave them of their sins.

Our faith is to be in Jesus Christ, not a particular pastor, teacher, building, or program. Furthermore, it is Jesus who we are to share with others. The big picture is Jesus! Most, if not all, that separates and divides the body of Christ is mended and restored in Jesus. A church that is not united has lost the big picture of sharing Christ with the world.

What is the result of a divided church? Paul stated that when the church is divided, the "cross of Christ [is] emptied of its power" (v. 17). The word *emptied* means to neutralize, or even worse, to falsify. When churches are divided, the message of Jesus becomes worthless to the ears of the world.

The good news is that Jesus is the Prince of Peace, and as we humble ourselves in his presence, all of the petty squabbling as well as the major arguments fade into the background. Pray that the peace of God will rule in your heart and church today.

QUESTIONS FOR REFLECTION

1. Have you ever been in a church that was full of strife and divisions? What were the issues? How did it make you feel? How effective was the church at reaching other people for Christ?

2. What happens when people in the church lose focus on what is really important? What steps can the church take to keep its focus? What steps can you take to keep your focus?

PRAYER FOR TODAY

Dear God, you have taught me how important it is to stay connected to a church and to do my part in keeping the church strong and united. Please forgive me for those times when I have been the problem at church. Help me to encourage and love other believers, helping them grow in their faith. Father, I give you the praise for all you are doing in my life. In Jesus' name. Amen.

WEEK 6

MINISTRY

RECOMMENDED READING

Total Quality Life, chapter 9, pages 156–159

Every member a minister; every saint a servant.

The greatness of a church is not measured by how many people attend the weekend services, but by how many people live out their faith during the week by using their spiritual gifts in ministry. God did not redeem us to set us on a shelf, collecting dust. God redeemed us to send us out into the world, collecting souls. Jesus came to serve, and you and I have been called to be like Jesus. Your faith in God will not grow without being stretched and strengthened through serving others. Total quality faith requires using your spiritual gift in ministry.

DAY 1

ACTS 1:6–11

The word *ministry* means to serve. As a follower of Jesus, you have been called to serve, thus, you are a minister. What are we to be doing as ministers? How are we to serve? In today's Scripture reading, Jesus gives us our ministry description.

After his resurrection, Jesus spent forty days teaching his followers, explaining how his life, death, and resurrection fit with the Old Testament, as well as describing what his followers were to be doing after he was gone. On one such occasion, the disciples asked Jesus if the time had come for him "to restore the kingdom to Israel" (v. 6).

Jesus replied by telling them that they were not to worry about times and dates. Rather, they were to wait for the promise of the Holy Spirit to come. And when the Holy Spirit did come, they would receive power and would be his witnesses all over the world, beginning at home (vv. 7–8). These were Jesus' final words. He had now given his followers instructions on ministry, and Jesus was "taken up before their very eyes" (v. 9).

To understand the full impact of Jesus' words, you have to go back to the night of his betrayal when he said to his disciples, "I tell you the truth, anyone who has faith in me will do what I have been doing. He will do even greater things than these, because I am going to the Father" (John 14:12).

Let those words sink in. As followers of Jesus, our ministry is to continue the ministry he began. And not only are we to continue his ministry, Jesus promises that we will do even greater things than he did. He healed the sick; raised the dead; gave sight to the blind; fed thousands of people; set captives free; spoke with clarity, power, and authority; and gave his life for others. Now he says we can and should be doing more and greater things.

How is that possible? It is possible because he sent his Holy Spirit (Acts 2), and since that day, the Spirit has indwelled, empowered, and equipped believers to continue the ministry of Jesus. It is through spiritual gifts that you and I are able to do greater things.

Embrace the Holy Spirit and use the gifts he gives you in ministry for him.

QUESTIONS FOR REFLECTION

1. Do you agree with the statement, "Every member a minister; every saint a servant"? Why or why not?

2. Do you think followers of Jesus today can do greater things than Jesus did in his day? Why or why not?

3. Do you know what your spiritual gifts are? Are you using your spiritual gifts in ministry for him?

PRAYER FOR TODAY

Dear Father, I can tell that this week is going to be a challenging one. Lord, I admit that much of my Christian experience has been about me and what you have done for me. I am now starting to realize that it is not about me, but about you and what I am doing for you in ministry. God, I pray that over the next few days you will show me how I can serve and what my spiritual gifts are. In Jesus' name I pray. Amen.

DAY 2

Romans 12:3–8

Being involved in ministry is vital for your faith to grow, but your ministry hinges on understanding spiritual gifts. Paul wrote, "Now about spiritual gifts, brothers, I do not want you to be ignorant" (1 Cor. 12:1). Just like then, many people today are ignorant about spiritual gifts, and ignorance is not bliss.

There are four primary passages about spiritual gifts in the New Testament. Over the next four days, we will look at each one. Today's passage is Romans 12:3–8. Stop and take time to read those verses.

God gives believers spiritual gifts to equip us to continue Jesus' ministry in today's world. Spiritual gifts are not for our enjoyment, but for our employment. We are to use them humbly, because we know we did nothing to earn them. Paul said, "Do not think of yourself more highly than you ought" (v. 3). God has given each of us a "measure of faith" (v. 3), and we are all part of his body (v. 5).

Paul stated, "We have different gifts, according to the grace given us" (v. 6). The words translated *gifts* and *grace* are similar. The Greek word translated *gifts* is *charisma* and the Greek word translated *grace* is *charis*. Paul was saying that we have varying grace gifts given by grace. In other words, spiritual gifts come from God and cannot be earned. Paul then mentioned seven specific gifts of grace (vv. 6–8). Whatever gifts God has given you, use them to the best of your ability in service to others.

The spiritual gift of prophecy is the ability to speak the Word of God. The main job of a prophet is to serve others by exposing sin, proclaiming righteousness, and calling people to repentance. If a person has the gift of prophesy, he or she should use it in "proportion to his [or her] faith" (v. 6), meaning in agreement with truth already revealed in Scripture.

The spiritual gift of service is the ability to demonstrate love by meeting practical needs. People who exercise this gift of grace are the true hands and feet of Jesus.

The spiritual gift of teaching is the ability to make the unchanging message of God understandable to others. People exercising this gift love to search out truths, sharing what they have learned with others.

The spiritual gift of encouragement is the ability to come alongside others, stimulating their faith and giving them courage to continue.

The spiritual gift of giving is the ability to entrust personal assets to others to advance the gospel. A person with this gift gives beyond a tithe, generously and liberally.

The spiritual gift of leadership is the ability to communicate goals and visions to the body of Christ in such a way that it motivates others to action. People who have this gift of grace are able to coordinate and motivate people to move toward common goals.

The spiritual gift of mercy is the ability to feel empathy and compassion for individuals who are going through distressing physical, mental, emotional, or spiritual problems. A person exercising this gift of grace considers it a privilege to enter into the sufferings of others.

Imagine what would happen if everyone in your church knew what their spiritual gifts were and exercised the gifts of grace in service and ministry to others!

QUESTIONS FOR REFLECTION

1. Of the seven gifts defined above, which one best represents you? Why?

2. What can you do this week in an attempt to use your spiritual gifts in service and ministry to others?

PRAYER FOR TODAY

Dear God, please show me what my spiritual gifts are. I want to serve you and minister to others. I want to do my part in building your kingdom. I pray for discernment and courage to step out in faith and use my gifts. Thank you for your gifts of grace. In Jesus' name I pray. Amen.

DAY 3

EPHESIANS 4:1–16

Have you heard of the 80/20 principle? There are several applications of this principle, but in the church it works this way: 80 percent of the work or ministry is performed by 20 percent of the people. Think what would happen if every person in the church were involved in ministry instead of just 20 percent.

Ministry is done through the power of the Holy Spirit and the gifts he has given every believer. The Holy Spirit has given you spiritual gifts that he wants you to use to further the kingdom. But not only do individuals have gifts of grace, Jesus has equipped the church with spiritual gifts as well. These gifts are known as office gifts, and they are given to equip the people in the church to continue the ministry of Jesus.

How do we continue the work of Jesus? Paul wrote, "It was [Jesus] who gave some to be apostles, some to be prophets, some to be evangelists, and some to be pastors and teachers" (v. 11). These five ministry gifts are roles people play within the body of Christ "to prepare God's people for works of service, so that the body of Christ may be built up" (v. 12). Let's take a closer look at these gifts.

An apostle is someone sent with a message. In the New Testament, the word was used in two ways. It referred specifically to the original twelve disciples of Jesus, plus Paul. The word was also used to refer more generally to individuals who spread the gospel in various locations, planted churches, and took leadership positions over groups of churches.

Jesus called the original apostles for a specific purpose, and used them in a unique way. They would always stand alone as the only ones who were chosen by Jesus to give birth to the church. How, then, is this gift used today? A person with the ministry gift of apostleship has been gifted by Christ with the special ability to extend the work of the church, opening new fields to the gospel and overseeing larger sections of the body of Christ.

In Romans, Paul mentioned the spiritual gift of prophecy. Here, he mentioned the spiritual gift of the office of a prophet. Within the church, a prophet warns people of sin, and calls God's people to repentance. The prophet reminds us of truths already in God's Word. A prophet can give insights and new understandings and warn us of what may happen in the future. However, prophecy should never be equated with God's revealed will found in the Bible, and all prophecy is subject to the authority of God's Word.

An evangelist is one who announces the gospel. The evangelist preaches Christ, keeps the message of Christ constantly before the church, and trains and encourages believers to share their faith with others.

The common word for *pastor* in Paul's day was *shepherd*. Paul used this word as a metaphor to describe those who take care of, lead, feed, and protect a local assembly of believers. The office of pastor is a grace gift God gives people in the body of Christ to assume a long-term personal responsibility for the spiritual welfare of a group of believers.

Again, in Romans Paul mentioned the spiritual gift of teaching. Here, he mentioned the spiritual gift of the office of teacher. Teachers serve the church by making the unchanging message of God understandable. Teachers clarify truths and keep the body of Christ from errors in doctrine.

These five gifts are offices or roles people play within the body of Christ to prepare others to be involved in ministry. They serve as trainers and resource people to equip those in the church for ministry. A person's ministry gift is what that person does within the body of Christ to build others up in their faith.

QUESTIONS FOR REFLECTION

1. What do you think of the 80/20 principle? Do you think it applies to your church?

2. In your church, who are the people who you think fill the offices of the church mentioned by Paul in Ephesians 4:11–13? Are you regularly praying for those individuals?

PRAYER FOR TODAY

Father, thank you for the things you are showing me this week. I pray for the ministry of my church. I pray for my pastor and for all the leaders in my church. Grant them wisdom and discernment as they lead the congregation. Thank you for the gifts you have given to my church. In Jesus' name. Amen.

DAY 4

1 CORINTHIANS 12:1–11

When spiritual gifts are discussed in the New Testament, it is always in the context of church unity. Spiritual gifts are meant to unite the body of Christ. They are not divisive, even though people's attitudes about them can sometimes be.

The apostle Paul wrote, "Now about spiritual gifts, brothers, I do not want you to be ignorant" (v. 1). Then, in verses 7–11, Paul mentioned nine spiritual gifts that he called a "manifestation of the Spirit" (v. 7). Often, in studying these gifts, people become sidetracked by arguing whether these gifts still exist today. But Paul's point was to explain the purpose of spiritual gifts. In verses 2–6, Paul mentioned four purposes.

First, spiritual gifts are a sign that God has redeemed you. Paul reminded the Christians in Corinth from where God had brought them. Before, they were being "led astray" (v. 2). But through God's grace, Paul said, "you were washed, you were sanctified, you were justified in the name of the Lord Jesus Christ and by the Spirit of our God" (6:11). The Holy Spirit is the seal of our relationship with God and the source of our spiritual gifts. It is the indwelling presence of the Holy Spirit that produces fruit; but it is the empowering presence of the Holy Spirit that ministers through spiritual gifts. When you use your spiritual gifts to serve others, you are giving evidence that God's grace has changed and redeemed you.

Second, spiritual gifts identify you with Jesus (v. 3). How do you know if a person is using a real or counterfeit spiritual gift? You know by what that person says about Jesus. A person who has the Holy Spirit and is using spiritual gifts in ministry cannot curse Jesus also.

Third, spiritual gifts are given to us for service in the body of Christ. Notice how verses 4–6 focus on the Trinity. The subject of verse 4 is God the Holy Spirit. The subject of verse 5 is God the Son or Lord. The subject of verse 6 is God the Father. Each plays a significant role in the distribution of spiritual gifts. Here is the point: Every believer has received spiritual gifts from the Holy Spirit that are to be used to continue the ministry of Jesus so that the kingdom of God is advanced on earth.

Finally, spiritual gifts demonstrate unity in diversity. Did you notice the word *same* in verses 4–6? In spite of the different gifts and variety of functions, we are all on the same team. Unity does not mean uniformity. Unity is using our diverse gifts to work together as a team to accomplish a common goal. Spiritual gifts were given so we could advance the kingdom of God together.

QUESTIONS FOR REFLECTION

1. Why do you think that spiritual gifts, which were meant to unite the body of Christ, have sometimes divided the body of Christ?

2. Of the four purposes of spiritual gifts listed in today's reading, which one do you think is the most important? Why?

PRAYER FOR TODAY

Dear God, today I pray for unity in the church. Not just in my local church, but unity in the entire church. I pray for unity in the body of Christ. Help me to do my part and to use my gifts to bring about that unity. Help me to use my spiritual gifts in ministry for you. In Jesus' name I pray. Amen.

DAY 5

1 PETER 4:1–11

Every member a minister; every saint a servant. You have been saved to serve. You have been redeemed to minister. You have been commissioned to continue the work of Jesus. And through spiritual gifts, you can change your world in the power of the Holy Spirit.

Do you know what your spiritual gifts are? Are you using your gifts of grace in ministry?

Today's Scripture is the last of four key passages in the New Testament dealing with spiritual gifts. In today's reading, Peter showed how gifts and ministry are connected.

There should be a stark contrast in our lives before we started following Jesus and after we started following him. Before we met Jesus, we lived for "evil human desires" (v. 2), but after, we live "for the will of God" (v. 2), even to the point that we sometimes experience abuse from others because we no longer participate in earthly things (vv. 3–6).

Peter admonished us to keep our minds clear and to be self-controlled so we can pray (v. 7). Our lives are to be marked by love and hospitality (vv. 8–9), and we are to use whatever spiritual gifts we have received "to serve others, faithfully administering God's grace in its various forms" (v. 10). The phrase "faithfully administering" (v. 10) indicates that we are stewards of God's grace and, as such, we don't own our spiritual gifts. They are gifts of God's grace for us to use as he wishes. Ministry means using your gifts of grace to faithfully distribute God's grace to others. That is our high calling.

Total quality faith involves getting involved in ministry and serving others. The happiest, most joyful, and most content you will ever be in your Christian life is when you discover and use your spiritual gifts in ministry.

How do you discover your spiritual gifts? You discover them best through trial and error. In other words, don't wait until you know what your gifts are before you use them in ministry. Rather, look at the needs around you, step out in faith, get involved in serving others, and determine by experience how God has gifted you.

Don't wait any longer. Grow and exercise your faith through ministry today.

QUESTIONS FOR REFLECTION

1. In what ways is your life different since you have started following Jesus? Have any of your old associates given you trouble because of your belief in Christ and the changes he has made in your life?

2. What do you think of the following definition of ministry: "Ministry is using your gift of grace to faithfully distribute God's grace to others"?

3. Why do you think more believers do not get involved in ministry?

PRAYER FOR TODAY

Lord, I praise and worship you. You have filled me with your grace and given me gifts of grace to be used for you. I pray I will be a good steward of the gifts you have given me. From this day forward, help me recognize opportunities to serve others by distributing your grace to them through the grace you have given me. Thank you for changing my life. I love you. In Jesus' name. Amen.